T0145002

Lead

Essential Lessons for
a Young Leader

Vanessa Gracia Cruz

WESTBOW
PRESS®
A DIVISION OF THOMAS NELSON
& ZONDERVAN

WestBow Press books may be ordered through booksellers or by contacting:

WestBow Press
A Division of Thomas Nelson & Zondervan
1663 Liberty Drive
Bloomington, IN 47403
www.westbowpress.com
1 (866) 928-1240

ISBN: 978-1-5127-8491-6 (sc)
ISBN: 978-1-5127-8490-9 (e)

Library of Congress Control Number: 2017906826

Print information available on the last page.

WestBow Press rev. date: 5/8/2017

*For the Gracia family, who made me who I am, and taught
me many of the lessons that I pass on through this book.*

*For my mom and dad, who set an example of
leadership, and gave me a legacy to carry.*

*And to Ru, Jessie, and JJ, my first team. Thank you for letting
me boss you around. It helped to develop my leadership skills!*

Foreword

L ead is a practical collection of ideas that will not only motivate young leaders, but serve as a starter-kit for leading. It contains basic, but very important principles that make up the first steps in successful leadership. Although it originates from a Christian perspective, its use does not exclusively stay within those boundaries. It transcends to those who want to lead in the marketplace as well. I personally recommend this book, because I see the incredible value that these practical lessons represent to our generation.

There are two things that make a successful leader. The first is a God-given ability to lead, and the second is guidance from other, more experienced leaders. Vanessa Gracia Cruz possesses both of these. Making her, if not an expert in the field of leadership, a definite voice of wisdom for the emerging generation of leaders of our time. I believe that her point of view is unique because she not only grew up in a family of leaders, but also had access to vast resources of wisdom that surrounded her in her childhood- being able to call some of today's most relevant and powerful leaders in Latin America her "aunts and uncles." My daughter, Vanessa, is a compass for a multitude of young people around the world. This guide will help them rise up and reach their destiny.

—Pastor Ruddy Gracia

Table of Contents

Introduction

I sometimes like to tell the story about how I aged twenty years in a day. I was a twenty-three year old, working part-time as my father's assistant, earning my MBA, and thinking I had all the time in the world before I'd have to figure out my next move. But in what seemed like the blink of an eye, I was the Chief Operating Officer of one of the largest and fastest growing churches in the United States. I was now directing a staff of over forty people, a ministry of thousands, and hundreds of home groups. I only had half a business degree, but I became the head of human resources, acting CFO, and Event Director. Yes, this all happened in one day, which also happened to be the day my mother passed away.

I'll back up a little so you can fully understand the story... My mother and father founded our home church when I was about two years old. Throughout my entire childhood, I watched them build this ministry. I saw first hand how it grew from a group small enough to fit in our first, one-bedroom apartment, to an organization that was literally impacting the world. I know that this experience laid the groundwork for my leadership. I grew up wanting to make an impact in people's lives. I was inspired by how my parents built teams from unlikely people. They'd believe in them, teach them, and motivate them, until these people were building teams of leaders themselves.

I remember being most impressed with my mom. My father was, and still is, the visionary, but my mom was the heartbeat of the operation; she kept everything going. My mother was in charge of the finances, the staff, and all of the operations. There was very little decision making that first didn't go through her. She was the time-keeper, planner, and strategist. She was my first, and greatest example of a strong, female leader. I was always impressed by how gracefully she moved from one task to another, and how people listened whenever she spoke. Even with all the things she had to do, her priority always remained teaching me how to do what she did. She'd slow down, and explain her tasks and teach me what she had learned from making mistakes at my age. Sometimes I can still hear her voice in my head whenever I have to make a big decision, and I can't help but wonder if somehow she had a clue that she was grooming me to one day assume her role.

In the summer of 2013, my mom got sick. It was a sudden illness, and three months later, she passed away. That was the day I refer to as the day I aged twenty years. My role changed from that of any normal, twenty-three-year-old student, to one that had taken my mother twenty plus years to earn. A void had been left in the organization that I loved, and I decided (albeit reluctantly) to step up and do my best to fill the gaping hole. Looking back, I'm not sure if I was temporarily insane, or if I hadn't realized the full weight of my mom's responsibilities. But I was motivated out of love for my mom and dad, and love for God's house. I couldn't stand the thought of the church potentially unraveling, and I knew my father couldn't lead it alone. It also helped that there was no one else volunteering for the job! Having no other choice is an incredible motivator in times of crisis. I stepped up to the plate, and began what was the most difficult season of my life.

Not only was I heart-broken, I didn't have a clue what I

was doing. I had lost my mother, my mentor, and my teacher. I was still finishing my degree, but was finding that what I learned in the classroom wasn't always practical to help me with the everyday challenges I was facing. Believe it or not, there is no class entitled "How to inherit an entire system of operations and not completely mess it up, while everyone is watching." For what seemed like a lifetime, I worked many long days and nights. I struggled with decision making, disgruntled employees, and felt the weight of leadership heavy on my shoulders. During that time, I honestly wasn't sure if I was going to last. I contemplated giving up nearly every day. It just seemed too difficult.

Thankfully, it wasn't long before a handful of great leaders took notice of my struggle, and began to advise me. They pointed me in the direction of useful leadership materials, and started me on what has now become a life-long journey of learning about leadership. They ignited a passion in me to learn how to lead the people in my organization, and how to overcome the obstacles that hindered me in the first season of my leadership. I began to devour book after book about personal development, time management, and leadership success. I discovered that leadership is a lot like riding a bike- you can start off wobbly, unsure, and off balance, but with time, you can learn to do it gracefully, and eventually even enjoy the ride.

It didn't happen overnight, but in time, I did learn to lead the organization. Today, I enjoy my role, my busy schedule, and all the ups and downs that come with them. I've earned the respect of the individuals who at first refused to listen to me because they thought I was just a "little girl." I am so thankful for the men and women who invested time into writing books that gave me both wisdom, and encouragement on this journey. Still, I wished that I had heard the perspective from someone my age. I noticed that all the authors and speakers I learned from were in their forties and older. While I appreciated their experiences, I wanted to hear from someone in the same season of life that I was in. I began to look for books that were specifically about leadership, written by someone in their twenties, but I couldn't find one. So, I wrote one.

This book is for anyone who is in a position of leadership, and isn't quite sure where to begin. Perhaps you have come into a new position in your ministry, or in your workplace. Maybe you have started your own venture as an entrepreneur. You may feel lost, or disoriented, and you may have even wondered if you are too young to be in leadership. If that's your case, I hope my story teaches you two things. The first is that you never know when you will be called upon to lead on a larger scale than you ever have, so you might as well learn now. Second, no matter how you begin, or what circumstances surround the start of your leadership, you can learn to lead well. This book is a compilation of the simplest, and most practical lessons I've learned throughout my leadership journey, and how to apply them regardless of your level of leadership. I hope that ignites in you a passion to become a lifetime learner of the craft, and inspires you to lead well, and be an excellent supervisor, manager, or mentor. More than anything, I hope it encourages you if you've gotten off to a rough start.

With Love,

UNDERSTANDING YOUR ROLE

The first step in becoming a leader is developing your own person. It is finding the balance between honoring those who led you, and learning to think for yourself. As children, we are taught to respect and obey our elders and do as we are told. This continues to be sound advice and a good practice at whatever age. However, a shift of responsibility begins to take place as we mature and become adults. This shift is an even greater challenge for those of us who assume positions of leadership as young adults. Our role changes from one of following directions carefree (knowing that someone else will be held accountable for the outcome) to being in a position of responsibility that requires accountability. Understanding this new role can be one of the greatest challenges for young leaders. It is much more comfortable to keep the status quo, and allow the "adults" to do the thinking. That is, until we realize that we have become the adults! And that we, as leaders, now have the responsibility to direct our teams and organizations.

When I came into my first position of leadership, I remember feeling overwhelmed and intimidated by the sense of duty. I no longer felt comfortable with quietly doing what I was told, but I hadn't yet found the confidence to implement changes in my new role as a leader. I had inherited a team of people who were all older than me, and I cringed at the thought of having to present an opposing view, needing to correct them, or proposing an idea I thought they might not like. Many of them had more experience than I did, and several had more influence with the rest of the team. Later on I'll address how I managed to gain their respect and influence them myself. The point I'm making is that at the beginning there were many occasions when my ideas were immediately shot down. I would propose an idea I had learned in business school or present the use of a new software that I had researched, and the entire room of people would be quick to tell me that I was wrong, that it wouldn't work, and that we should stick to what had already been established. At first, it seemed easier to let them have the final say. I'd reason that they were the "adults" and the "professionals" and that things would work out better if I'd be a peace-maker and leave it up to them. For some reason, I was already in my twenties, but I felt as though I wasn't as "adult" as they were.

That was until I started realizing that the organization wasn't doing as well as it could be. For example, I observed that my team's resistance to the use of a new software created bottle-necks, slowed down processes, and wasted time. I began to see that some of my ideas would be beneficial. And I realized that when we failed as a team, it was a reflection of my leadership ability. I was the one that would be held accountable, because I was in the lead. It didn't take long before I knew I had to speak up, and be courageous enough to act like the leader, or I wasn't going to be a very successful one.

It can be easier for us young leaders to yield to strong opinions and forceful voices because of our age. We are often afraid to make changes because we lack confidence in ourselves. Sometimes we question why, out of all the people who could have been chosen to be in the position we hold, did we end up with the job. And unfortunately, sometimes we allow that question to distract us from our obligations as leaders. You see, a leader's job isn't to determine what makes him or her worthy of leadership. Neither is it to sit back passively and allow others to bully him or her into making decisions against their better judgment. Leaders must lead their teams to the best of their ability and this will require asserting themselves and at times making changes.

When I took my first leadership position, I thought I would do things as my mother and father had done them. They were my role-models and they knew what they were doing. With all their years of experience, there was no doubt, they built a solid organization. However, in my time as a leader I had to discern for myself what part of their legacy I was called to continue and what I might be called to change. Be assured, none of what I'm writing devalues or discredits any of their excellent work. I never challenged the core values or convictions they instilled in me, but I did challenge practices, ideas, and processes that had become outdated.

Of course, there were times when it was hard for the team to accept these changes. I've learned that some people prefer the familiar even if they know it isn't the best option, simply because change can be scary and uncomfortable. But innovation stimulates growth. As much as I wanted to carry on my parent's legacy, I realized that if I wasn't causing the organization to grow, I wasn't doing justice to their legacy. I discovered that there was little value in leading others to do something that I myself couldn't fully endorse. Simply put, you should ultimately believe in your decisions and understand your rationale for making them. Sometimes the best decision may be unpopular, but when you are convicted that your decision is the right one and that beyond your pride, or personal feelings, it is still in the best interest of all, you must stick to your position.

By writing this, I by no means wish to imply that we rebel against the direction and established rules and systems of our present leaders. In places where someone else is in charge, my advice is to allow them to lead and respect their position. Here, I am talking about the things you are in the position to control. As a leader, you may take heat for whatever decision you make. After you have weighed the opinions of others, go with what you truly believe to be best.

Remember, that there are many instances in which the leader has the bigger picture in mind. Members of your team will have a lot to offer, especially those with years of experience, but they can often be looking only at their area, and considering only how decisions affect them. To become a leader with integrity, you will need to learn how to move forward with a decision knowing that you did your best and followed what you believed in your heart to be best for the organization as a whole. I believe that learning to be confident in decision making will not only make us better leaders but better people. I would encourage you to be respectfully assertive and speak up instead of keeping silent about processes or systems that you know should be changed.

At the end of the day, the first step to becoming a leader is understanding that if you were capable enough to make it to leadership, then you are capable of growing into leadership. Recognize that speaking up is more than something you should do; it is your duty as a leader to do so. Twenty years from now, you may look back on the decisions you make for your organization with pride, or you may realize that you made mistakes. Either way, you will want to own those decisions. You will want to be someone who resisted simply following the paths of others. Instead, you will have been someone who paved the way- a leader.

EARNING YOUR INFLUENCE

The first and biggest challenge I faced as a young leader was earning respect. At the beginning of your leadership role, it's important to understand that people will not follow you because you were endorsed by the leader who gave you the position. People don't follow leaders because they hold high level degrees or a résumé filled with prestigious corporations and titles. If you try to manipulate or coerce people to follow they will resist and lose respect for you. No one is a fan of a twenty-something-year-old immature go-getter trying to forcefully take charge and change everything. Leadership is influence. It is the ability to direct a person or group of people to move in a specific direction, and have them help you accomplish goals for the organization. Regardless of your place in the organizational chart or how much power you have, you will need to influence people in order to get things done. Respect will have to be earned in order to have this influence. It takes time and a lot of hard work to have your voice be the one people want to listen to. I have seen many young leaders try to cut corners and fail to build relationship, forcing their will on the people they lead. If you take that route, you may be able to have them follow your direction today but they will never really be supportive. If you can't get them to back you up they will never consider you to be their leader. You will be considered the "son-of", "assistant-of", or "replacement-of" the previous leader but never the real deal.

When I first became an executive, I learned quickly how little a title does for you in leadership. In a short time, I went from being my father's assistant, a part-time job I held while working on my master's degree, to being in charge of the department heads, each one being individuals in their forties and fifties. I had everything I needed: an MBA, years of experience in the church, and my father, their pastor, who had placed me there and "strongly suggested" that everyone respect me. But I couldn't get them to listen to a word I said! Most of my ideas were rejected. I was interrupted almost every time I started to speak. I had a position, but I hadn't earned their respect and therefore had little influence. In their defense, let's look at it from their perspective. They had worked years to get where they were and this *young girl* was coming in to try and tell them what to do. They hadn't been convinced that I cared about them or knew what I was talking about. I had to earn their support and the backing they would eventually give me. Today, that team of leaders is my strongest asset. When I want to implement a new idea, I don't hesitate to take it to them and know that they will be supportive. They will even follow at times when they don't agree, because they have learned to trust me. It required intentional effort, and did not happen from one day to the next. Here are some *do's* and *don'ts* of earning your place of influence within an organization or a team.

DO: Get some wins

If you want the team to listen to your ideas, you'll need to demonstrate to them that your ideas actually work. They need to see your successes and victories, preferably ones that are mutually beneficial. At first, you may have to earn those successes on your own while your team is cautious about following your direction or challenges your authority. Do something to make their lives easier. Serve them. Make a plan and carry it out. When you say you are going to do something, follow through. The problem with many young leaders is that they seem flaky, inexperienced or like they haven't worked a day in their lives. So, get some experience under your belt, before you make radical changes. Don't be discouraged if it takes people a while to get behind you. Most people need time to decide if they want to follow someone or not. So, be consistent, and monitor your progress. Showing results is the surest way to show your team that you are trustworthy.

DON'T: Be a know-it-all

People appreciate a leader who can admit it when he or she is wrong. Most of us have a hard time accepting a person who throws around their degrees or number of years in a field just to get their way. Be humble and flexible. If your idea is good, it will eventually stand on its own. If it's not a good idea, don't be afraid to toss it. People will respect you for being a team player who considered someone else's idea if it was better than yours. The important thing to remember is that you don't need to be perfect so long as you are purposed. Be consistent and you'll start to notice the difference.

DO: Connect with your team

Your team is not an ocean. They are not one big mass or body. They are individuals and if you treat them as such, they will find it easier to respect you. If you don't, they they may be inclined to stay disconnected. If you don't know them, how can you know what is best for them? Find ways to connect to people one-on-one. Know their names. Ask about their families. Remember their birthdays. You may struggle to connect with that one team member who refuses to recognize the effort you're putting into building a relationship with them. But you will find that knowing how to relate to them will help you learn the best approach to presenting ideas and strategies.

DON'T: Throw tantrums

You don't want your team to see you as a bratty, snotty-nosed kid. So, don't act like one. There is no need for yelling, screaming or storming out of rooms. Old school leaders may have thought that this kind of behavior was a display of authority. But, it actually demonstrates a lack self-control and makes you look immature. Always keep a level head. If an argument ensues, take a break from the meeting until you have cooled off. Use logic and reason to show why you are right, not your temper. It is better to accept defeat on a certain issue but remain calm, mature, and consistent. Eventually, that in itself will earn you their admiration.

BUILDING YOUR TOOLBOX

Leadership, like a craft, can only be skillfully exercised by using the right tools. In the same way that no great artist can do without his brushes, canvases, or paint, it is important for leaders to equip themselves with the tools to execute to the best of their abilities. No one is born a leader, *leadership is mostly learned.* Meaning you don't have to rely on what you already know or your natural talents in order to be a great leader. John C. Maxwell says, "In 25 years, anyone can become a great leader, the secret is in their daily agenda."[1] Successful leaders are those that have made themselves lifelong learners of the craft. Those that dedicate the time and energy on a daily basis to expand their "toolbox" of leadership.

The more of the essential skills you cultivate and develop, the better leader you will be. Below are some of the tools in my toolbox that, over the years, have helped me get the job done. Consider adding these to your toolbox as well.

A Group of Advisors

Have conversations with people that can teach you how to be better at your craft. Raw talent is good but cannot compare to what we can learn from experienced leaders who have literally "been there, and done that." It is incredible how many leadership mistakes are repeated over and over simply because the new leaders never took the time to ask any questions! So, ask! Find people who have done the things you want to do and invite them to lunch or coffee, and ask them for a few minutes of their time. You don't need a formal agreement with this person, and they may not always need to become your mentor. That might actually discourage those who are too busy for such a commitment. Simply ask questions. Very often, you will learn a lot, avoid making big mistakes, and gain from their experience, all from a simple conversation. You don't need to limit yourself to only one advisor, either. You can have a number of people who speak into your life, offer you advice and answer questions you may have on different matters according to their area of expertise.

A Support Team

Chances are, your goals cannot be accomplished by you alone. And, even if you could reach them, they would be so much better if combined with the strengths of other key people who can add value to your vision. I'll use myself as an example. I'm great at writing content, but I need the input of people who know how to design, print, code, and give creative feedback. I have linked up with a team of people who believe in my vision enough to lend a hand. How did I do this? I just asked! You'd be amazed how many people would love to invest in your vision. After all, leadership is about getting people to do just that!

A Resilient Attitude

A resilient attitude can also be defined as the ability to fail-forward. By this I mean that even if you've technically failed, you've learned from your failure and as a result are propelled forward. As perplexing as this may sound, leadership and failure go hand in hand. You may fail on a large scale, or you may fail very often on a small-scale, with decisions that you later realize were not the right ones. The point is to develop the ability to fail-forward.

There is something to be learned from every setback and painful situation resulting from a mistake. The key is to discern what you can learn. Most leaders are natural visionaries and when they experience failure, they immediately look to the future. While this is a great quality, it is also important to take a brief look back and reflect on the failure to determine what can be learned from it.

LESSON 4

DEVELOPING ESSENTIAL HABITS

I despise New Year's resolutions. I hate this process because I've never seen the need for a date on the calendar to determine when to begin what we were already supposed to be doing. I do, however, understand how deciding to turn a new page can do wonders for our attitudes and habits. As much as I despise resolutions, I love the atmosphere of a new beginning. Every January you can almost smell it in the air; people get ready to take on new challenges. Now *that* I can get on board with! If there is one thing I have learned, it's this: successful people have good habits. They do positive things on a consistent basis that not only cause them to progress towards their goals, but also to grow and develop as people. So, if this book inspires you, don't wait to implement what you learn. Begin now to cultivate habits that will improve your leadership skills and grow you as a person. Here are five habits that I push myself to adhere to, regardless of the time of year.

Plan

Planning is like doing your homework; no one wants to do it but, if you do, you'll do better on the test. In this case, the test being your work, your family, and your overall productivity. You will do better if you become a good planner. Think ahead about what you want to accomplish throughout the week, rather than just letting it fly by. Block out time for things that are truly important. And, I can't emphasize this enough, get a planner! At first it may seem restricting, to think about things beforehand and plan. But planning actually frees your mind to create, envision and dream. It also saves you so much time. Time will seem to stretch if you plan your steps to avoid running around in circles.

Think

Take some time every day to think. Yes, this is serious. Not enough people, especially young people, take time to reflect and analyze their lives or their situations. Set time apart to think. *What are the things I should be doing that I am not? Do I love what I do? Do I love how I'm doing it? Should I change course? If I continue on this path, will I end up where I want to be?* It takes thought to be intentional about life, and it takes being intentional to lead.

Grow

Force yourself to learn something new every day. Develop the habit of dedicating time to your own personal growth, even if it's just 20 minutes a day. Stephen Covey calls it "sharpening the saw."[2] Take time to invest in the assets that make you, *you.* Focus on making your strengths, even stronger. If you have a talent, practice and use it. If you have an inclination, learn about it and grow in it. Many people miss the chance to be great at something because they are satisfied with being good.

I believe every leader needs a concrete growth plan. What are the things you are going to do each day to expand your skill-set? It's not enough to let time pass by and expect growth to come on its own. Remaining idle does not build your character, improve your skills or enhance your talent. In leadership, there are countless skills to develop and it requires an investment of time. Map out a strategy. For me, some facets of my plan include reading one book a month, and attending at least 2 conferences a year. This keeps me constantly developing, growing, and learning. Because I also want to grow spiritually, I dedicate at least 20 minutes a day to studying the Bible using a devotional or commentary that will give me greater understanding of what I'm reading.

Cut

If something isn't working, cut it out of your life. If you're serious about your dreams, distraction and waste should be two things you won't tolerate. You most likely have all the energy and time you need to accomplish your goals but may be spending them on the wrong things. Make a habit out of prioritizing as you plan. The two go hand-in-hand. Get to the more important things first. I once spent a week writing down everything I did *(everything)*. Then, I looked back to see if what I spent my time doing was worth it. I loved the process so much that I periodically do this exercise. If you can't find time for something important, look again at how you spend your time and there may be an activity you can cut.

Act

Decide to be a person who acts rather than reacts. The ability to initiate, separates leaders from followers. It's incredible what can be accomplished by someone who chooses to be proactive about their dreams. Instead of stagnating in disappointment or the hardships you've experienced, actively seek out the help, tools, people, or resources you need to accomplish your goal. We all love movies where the hero or heroine with a huge disability finds a way to win a gold medal or a Nobel Prize against all odds. However, we don't realize how often we let our own "disabilities" or simple procrastination, stop us from overcoming small odds and achieving our dreams. Make a habit of taking action on a goal every day. Do something to inch towards your dream, and start on new creative ideas as soon as they strike you.

L E S S O N 5

GOAL SETTING

I want to emphasize that goal-setting is of utmost importance. It's one of those concepts that everyone seems to agree is important yet in reality most people don't practice. Most people have dreams, but don't see how goals and objectives can be used as a ladder to achieve those dreams. By setting concrete goals and making a plan to reach them, we ensure that at the end of the year, month, or week that we are actually closer to our dreams, rather than regretting the fact that we aren't getting anywhere.

I'll be honest, this used to be a huge weakness of mine. Instead of setting goals, I did the most ineffective thing people do -- I made resolutions. A resolution is something you "resolve" to do, but it differs from a goal in that there is no definition of a desired outcome. It's like stating "I am going to start a blog" without strategizing how you are going to do it or determining exactly what your blog or project will look like. Everyone makes resolutions at one point or another, but this isn't goal setting. Unfortunately, it's more like wishful thinking and most of the time, it stays a simple wish and never gets done.

A resolution becomes a goal once you define your desired outcome. It is a concrete target like "by a specific date I want to have a fully functioning site, with at least one blog post." Now, you have something to work towards. In the months leading up to your goal's deadline you'll know you need to write at least one post, begin taking pictures, putting together your design, and checking off all the steps in your plan. This is the beauty of goal setting. Not only will it help you get more done, but if done correctly, setting goals can also help you create a road map of the year. Using this road map will help you make the most of your time. The goals that you set for your life help you determine the goals for your years, months, and days. In essence, it is like the inverted pyramid diagram below:

GOALS
What do I want to
do in my lifetime?

YEARLY GOALS
What do I need to do this year to
be closer to the life goal?

MONTHLY GOALS
How am I going to advance on my
yearly goals this month?
What steps am I taking?

WEEKLY GOALS
What do I have to do
this week to accomplish my
monthly goals?

DAILY GOALS
How can I work on
my weekly goal
today?

See how that works? Your goals, as I mentioned before, should work like a ladder towards your dreams. When we learn how to *use* our goals, we are able to ensure that we are heading in the direction we want. To do this, first we have to take some time to think about who we want to be, and project what we want for our life in the future. As you begin your goal-setting process, ask yourself the following questions:

Who do I want to be in 5-10 years?

What is my ultimate career goal?

What do I want to accomplish by the end of my life?

What is the next step in my personal development?

Even if you don't know the answers to all these questions, you can still set goals based on what you do know. If you want to be a doctor for example, perhaps your next step would be completing the first credits of your associate's degree. If the next step in your personal development is to spend more time with your family, then your first goal might be "I am going to spend one night a week with my family for the entire year." You can then use that goal to set your monthly and weekly goals. Each month, for example, you will pull out your calendar and schedule four dates you will dedicate to family time. Each week, you will confirm that date and on that day it will become one of your goals for the day. Goal setting should be an ongoing process, something you do every single day. This is how you ensure that you are actually accomplishing the goals you have set. At the end of the year, you may find that you have missed one or two of those family days, but I guarantee you will have had a lot more of them than you did the previous year!

Setting Measurable Goals

Once you have taken the time to explore the kind of goals you want to set, the next step is making sure the goals are achievable. For this, they will need to be measurable and *unbiased*. When something is unbiased, it means that it is not influenced by feelings or opinions but represented by facts. In order for you to set successful goals, you'll need to make sure your goals can be measured by fact, not feelings. I gave an example of a goal to accomplish a number of credits for a degree. That can be measured. At the end of the year, you won't be able to say "I *feel* like I did really well on that goal." You will have factual evidence that shows you either accomplished the goal or didn't.

You may wonder why I place so much emphasis on this. Here's why: objectivity is a way to win the battle against ourselves. You see, in general we tend to be too lenient with ourselves when it comes to goals. We tend to bring feelings into it and give ourselves a break when we know we have a lot going on. In this sense, we can all be our own enemies. We make excuses for ourselves. Setting measurable goals and putting them down on paper holds us accountable. By doing this, we apply a higher standard to our personal development. Great leadership begins with mastering this skill. Because, after all, if we can't do this for ourselves how can we do this for our teams?

Before you read on, I encourage you to take a few minutes to put each one of your goals to the test of objectivity and make adjustments if needed. Then, I recommend writing them down and putting your list in a place where you will see it every day. This will help to keep you on track. Ask yourself these questions about your goals:

Does my goal have a deadline?

A goal without a deadline is not a goal– it's wishful thinking. Make sure you set a time frame for when your goal needs to be completed. Remember, we are trying to win a battle against ourselves- without a set time frame we leave room for procrastination and can allow time to pass without making any progress.

Is there a way to recognize success?

Our goals should be specific and measurable so that we can recognize our victories. Try to avoid being overly broad or vague. For example, "this year I'll watch less TV" is too general. Whereas, "this year, I will only watch TV on two nights a week" is a measurable outcome.

Make sure there is a way to measure your progress. This way if you're falling behind, you'll know if you need to buckle down and give yourself a pep-talk. If your goal is the completion of a project, make sure you take time to envision all aspects of the project.

Are they realistic?

Goal setting is not the time to wish or fantasize. We want to be honest with ourselves and recognize our limitations. If we set unrealistic goals, we are only setting ourselves up to fail. Make sure your goals are consistent with your present life circumstance. If they are not, make a stepping-stone goal– a goal that gets you a little closer to where you need to be in order to hit the ultimate target. If, for example, your goal involves opening a business, which requires significant capital that you don't yet have, make your stepping-stone goal to start acquiring the capital. Whenever I want to double check if a goal is realistic, I think of all the steps it would take to accomplish that goal. If all the steps can be accomplished in the year, it becomes one of my year's goals. If I cannot reach the ultimate goal within the year, then I choose one of the steps. Essentially, I make my initial goal a "multi-year goal."

Are they within your control?

A goal, by definition, is something we can accomplish. This is what separates it from a wish. We may wish that certain situations change in our family or that the guy we have a crush on asks us out on a date, but we should definitely not make those things our goals. We should avoid making goals out of things that require other people to change their mind or do something out of the ordinary. Unless you have made an agreement with that person to do something together. Remember, you cannot control anyone but yourself. So, make sure your goals are things you have the power to accomplish, even if the rest of the world stays exactly as it is. These are *your* goals.

LEARNING TO PRIORITIZE

There is always someone or something demanding our attention. Responding to these demands can keep us busy all the time. The problem is that busyness doesn't always equal effectiveness. You can be busy and realize at the end of the day that in spite of expending all your energy, you didn't get any closer to achieving your goals. You were active, you just weren't intentional about your activity and you are not alone! One of the hardest skills for leaders to grasp and implement is how to prioritize. Of course, we all believe that prioritizing is important, we just don't actually put it into practice. The result is that we don't make the most of our time. Being effective means having to be cautious about what we allow onto our to-do lists and calendars. If we aren't cautious, we can waste a lot of valuable time doing things that either weren't necessary, or weren't of any value. Before you let something creep onto your list, making you even busier than you already are, ask yourself a few questions. Here's a list to consider:

Is this task necessary?

This may seem obvious, but many times I have ended up with tasks on my list or in my planner only to realize that if I thought it through for a few more minutes, I could have found a way to eliminate some steps or solve the problem in more time-efficient way.

Before you decide to shoot out the door and do something, make sure it really has to be done. Always remember to ask: how does this contribute to my goals? Tasks that require time and effort but do not directly benefit your overall goal may be wasting a lot of your time! I'm guilty of having a lot of "great ideas" for activities that I believe can be self-enriching. But, upon further consideration, I sometimes realize that the activity will distract me, and that the possible gain is not significant or valuable. Being effective means understanding you do not have an infinite amount of time, so spend it only on what really counts!

Does this task have to be done right away?

Many leaders are initiators and like to get things done right away. We have to be careful not to get so caught up in seemingly urgent tasks that we lose track of more important responsibilities. For example, often when I'm in my office I'll get a call about an urgent matter that will require my attention. It can be very tempting for me to drop what I'm doing and go put out the fire. But, I've learned that when I do that it takes a lot of time to refocus to my original task. Not only that but, if I let myself, I will spend my whole day running back and forth between one office to the other having spontaneous meetings or thinking *for* my team rather than giving them the opportunity to solve the problem on their own. I would never get any work done! I've learned that sometimes it's ok to roll something over to the next day or week if it's going to derail me from accomplishing something that needs to be done today.

Am I the best person for the job?

Here's a blow to our egos, leaders– the fact that we are in the lead doesn't automatically make us the best person for every job. Some tasks are an opportunity to challenge, teach or equip someone on your team. You may find they are actually more naturally gifted in that area than you are. Too many leaders try to do everything themselves and end up overwhelmed, with a team that is begging for more responsibility. Every once in a while, it's ok to let someone else take charge even if there is a possibility they will fail. This is also an opportunity to learn delegation. Remember that as a leader, you will never be able to accomplish greater things if you cannot learn to delegate your smaller tasks to someone else. Always ask yourself: *does this activity have to done by me? Can I ask someone else on my team to take this on?* If the answer is "yes" this task should not be on your list. Hand it over and put it on theirs. Occupy your list only with things that are necessary for YOU to do in order to reach your goals.

When assuming a new leadership role, many of us tend to take on too much, and don't delegate enough of the workload to our teams. Whether the motivation is humility, insecurity or something else, we make the mistake of taking on a greater part of the workload and as a result neglect to develop other leaders within our team. This contributes to our feeling of being overwhelmed by stress and disappointment that everything we wanted to accomplish, didn't get done. You hurt yourself and your team when you do the tasks that you should be delegating to someone else. They aren't learning and you aren't teaching, so you both miss out on fulfilling your roles.

One of my personal mentors once brought to my attention that there were a lot of things I wasn't accomplishing because I was spending my time doing other people's jobs. Because of me, my team members weren't able to shine, and I couldn't rise to the next level of responsibility. Before assigning yourself a task, consider if someone else might do it better. If the answer is no, it's your job, get to work! If the answer is yes, your responsibility becomes to find the most adequate person to fill the need. Our duty is to ensure each member of the team is focusing on his or her highest area of impact, including ourselves.

What if I just say *no*?

It's often the case that as a leader you will be invited to every meeting, conference call, be part of too many email streams and text message groups in the organization. Some will expect you to decide on matters of extreme importance at the drop of a hat in the middle of the hallway. They may call you on your family vacation asking questions that can easily be answered by someone else. Learn to guard your valuable time and your sanity by placing boundaries. Unless you learn to say *no*, a boundary on your accessibility will not be set. This does not mean that I am not flexible in emergencies or respond to a team member that is stumped and asks for help. However, I must set boundaries to protect my own productivity. I do not go to every meeting I'm invited to spontaneously. I ask people to respect my time by making an appointment. This way, when I meet with them I can devote my full attention to the matter at hand, do research if necessary, and finish my scheduled work.

I do not answer every question that is asked of me on the spot. Often I ask people to email me with their questions and suggestions, which allows me to think before I respond. I may also direct them to another person equally capable of listening to them and making the decision. When someone walks into my office and I am busy, I politely ask them to return when I am able to attend to them properly. In short, sometimes I say *no, not now, or not me.* If I didn't do this, I would spend every minute of my day in meetings or on the phone and I would never dream, plan, or lead. I am here to serve, but within the reasonable boundaries I have set to protect my time, my health, and my emotional well-being.

Again, your job is to lead, to teach others to solve problems, think for themselves, and assure that things run smoothly even when you are not present. Be aware of things like these that make you less productive and stress you which may lead to burn out.

CREATING CULTURE

As a leader, it is your responsibility to create culture. The culture of an organization is dependent on what the leader (or leaders) promote as important or of value. Your team will take their cues from you, and people outside of your organization (whether they are clients or members of a congregation) will take their cues from your team. The culture and values that you establish will define how the public perceives you. In everything you do, whether you realize it or not, you are promoting what is acceptable, what is important, and how you expect your team to perform. This is a lot of responsibility, right? I promise I'm not trying to scare you. I do, however, want to make sure you understand the importance of being intentional in everything you do as a leader.

One thing many developing leaders struggle with is decision-making. Tough decisions such as determining which issues to address, or how to allocate resources can be made easier by defining the values of an organization. What are the things that are important to you as a leader? What are the things you want your organization to value? No organization can excel at everything at once, but its culture will be a reflection of whatever you value most. So choose wisely. We know, for example, that a company like McDonald's values speed, while another company like Chick-Fil-A may put a higher value on customer service. Craig Groeschel, one of my favorite speakers on leadership, recommends defining your values by asking yourself two questions: *What do I love? What breaks my heart or makes me righteously angry?*[3]

These kinds of intentional questions define your personal values, and help you determine what values you want to instill in your organization. For example, my company, Millennial Grace, was founded on my passion to help young leaders and businesses grow. I loved becoming a leader and learning the skills that made me successful, and I wanted to share that with others. As a result, my team and I value attitudes that reinforce what I believe leads to success. Excellence, efficiency, and organization are examples of these values. Because everyone understands these values, everything that is consistent with them is promoted amongst us. Anything that is not, I will find a way to change or improve in order to align with our values. If you are wondering what the culture of your organization will be, ask yourself the following questions about your organization, team, or brand:

What do we reward here?

Regardless of what you *say* your values are, your actions will always speak louder than words. So, ask yourself: *What do I reward my team for? What do they know they can do to be promoted in this group? Do I allow manipulative behavior as a way to get ahead? Do I celebrate cutting corners when it means sacrificing excellence?*

If you want your team to exhibit specific behaviors, reward them only when their behaviors are consistent with the culture you are trying to establish. I've seen many businesses and even ministries that say they value integrity, but reward team members who lie to vendors or to each other. These leaders are sending a message that is more powerful than words.

What do we ignore here?

Sometimes silence is just as powerful as verbal reinforcement. The things you ignore also send an important message about what you value. When you've got a lot on your plate, it can be tempting as a leader to ignore small issues such as tardiness, or inefficiency. Just be aware that every time you ignore something, you are passively reinforcing it. Over time, your team members will develop the idea that "it's no big deal" and act accordingly.

What gets the most of my attention?

Where do you spend the most time, resources, and overall attention? What do you talk about the most? What meetings are you obviously more enthusiastic about? The answer to those questions should come easily to you, and you may be surprised how easily they are answered by the rest of your team. As they get to know you as a leader, they'll learn what tugs at your heart, and most likely they will invest in these things as well. That's a good thing! But beware of being imbalanced. There may be some values you should make a greater effort to emphasize. They may not be the ones that interest you the most, but if they reflect the culture you are trying to create, they must be addressed. For example, not every leader likes to discuss budget cuts, but if stewardship is one of your core values, you may need to from time to time.

What do I model?

Lastly, what do you model? As much as I'd like to tell you that the whole "do as I say, not as I do" thing works, it doesn't. The truth is, no matter what you reward, invest in, or push, if you don't practice what you preach, your team will believe that it's not as important as you let on. The responsibility of living your values simply comes with the territory of being a leader. If there is an area that you are having a hard time living up to, try re-evaluating whether or not it's really important to you. There's a chance that maybe it isn't, and you were simply holding onto it out of habit or because it was important to someone else. However, if it is still something you value, make sure you are modeling it for your team. Truly exceptional leaders are those who are able to inspire their teams to believe in the organization's values as much as the leader does. The only way to do that is by showing that you honestly believe what you say.

LEADING WHEN YOU'RE NOT IN CHARGE

I want to take some time to address those of you who desire to change the culture in your ministry or at your job, but are unable to, because you aren't all the way at the top. You've got a manager, CEO, or senior pastor to answer to, and you don't call all the shots. For now, you think all you can do, is do the best you can and wait until the day they move on, retire or the day you get their job. Realistically, most leaders are not at the absolute top of the organizational chart. In any given organization there will be dozens of second and third tier administrators, and especially if you are in your 20s and 30s this is probably where you find yourself.

There are unique challenges to being second or third in command. Sometimes you identify with top management, and other times understand the perspective of general employees. You are the middle manager and you have enough responsibility to want to pull your hair out, yet not enough control to change the things that stress you. It can be exhausting. But I assure you that you do not just have wait until it's your turn. There is so much you can do from the position you presently hold. It's not at all easy, but change is possible. You will simply have to do it the smart way.

This is a very personal chapter for me because while I am the head of my own ventures, I still work under my dad at the church he and my mom founded. We are two different people, with different experiences, from two totally different generations. We definitely don't always see eye to eye. But at the end of the day, *he* is my leader. I don't have it all figured out when it comes to working alongside my father, but over the years and through a lot of prayer, I've learned some keys to making it work.

I'll warn you, this won't be the easiest chapter to read. The truth is, leaders want to do just that—lead. It's difficult to put your better judgment aside and accept someone else's. I've seen many young leaders end up bitter, or quit their organizations because they couldn't balance following their leader with leading their followers. If you are in this spot, I hope I can encourage you not to give up. As you read through the rest of this chapter, keep in mind that influence is a two-way street. You may be instrumental in helping your leader grow. Here are a few keys to successfully leading as a middle manager:

Lead and be led

Most young leaders love to lead, but are very uncomfortable being led. However, you don't have an option if you aren't the top leader of the organization. This will continue to be true no matter how hard you fight for control or disagree. You'll need to accept that this person is in the lead, learn to respect them, and allow them to give direction. If you are wise, you will learn to find joy and rest in the fact that they can teach you, and that the whole weight of the organization does not fall on you (trust me, that's not a small thing).

I've seen too many young leaders start at the bottom of an organization, and work themselves up to a place of influence, working closely with the CEO, or senior pastor. When they reach this level, however, they become disillusioned, disrespectful or outright defiant. They would say it is because their leader is stubborn, ignorant, or inadequate. The truth is that there is no excuse for this type of behavior. The more your team sees you dishonor your superiors, the less value they will give to honoring you. So, lead and be led. Let your leader be to you, who you hope to be to your team. Accept their vision, direction, and correction because learning to follow is part of becoming a leader.

Make peace with your borders

You may have lost sleep over some of the things in the organization that truly worry you, but your leader refuses to change. If that's you, you'll need to learn, as I have, to accept the boundaries of your authority. If there are things your leader doesn't want you to touch, let them go. If there are situations beyond your control, accept them. At the end of the day, they are your leader's responsibility, and you will drive yourself nuts if you try to hold yourself accountable to everything that goes on. Here's a saying that I chant to myself when my leader has said "no" or asked me to stay out--"not my circus, not my monkeys." In other words, if it's beyond the scope of my responsibilities, I've got to let it go, and make peace with the borders I've been given.

Influence works both ways

Just as you can influence those under you, you can also influence those above you. We should never forget the privilege it is to be second in command, because our leaders often look to us for input. If we are wise, we will realize that the best thing we can do for both our leaders and the organization is to use our influence to help them lead.

Each one of the principles in this book about gaining the respect of your team can also be used to gain the trust of your leader. Don't be stubborn, throw tantrums, or be sneaky. People can sense this and your leader is no exception. If your leader is reluctant to listen to you, ask yourself why that might be. It's possible you have some work to do on your own leadership to gain their respect. Once you do, you'll reap the immense benefits of having traction with your leader. If you join forces with them instead of struggling, you'll find that your job is a lot easier. My father and I don't always see eye to eye, but I've earned enough of his respect to have him consider my ideas, and try out systems even when he doesn't agree with them. By gaining his trust, I've been able to bring about positive change to the organization, and I know that both he and my team appreciate that.

Over-communicate

No one likes to be micro-managed, so if your leader is a little controlling you might be tempted to communicate less, in order to do what you want. You probably don't do this maliciously; you just want to be able to finish something before your leader butts-in. I urge you, however, to fight this temptation! The less you communicate, the more likely they will increase their oversight. Not only that, it diminishes your opportunity to influence because it can make you look sneaky, even if you aren't. Face it, no leader likes the idea of someone in their organization making moves without them knowing. You probably don't like it if your team does it to you, so don't do it to your boss, even if you think that what you are doing is right.

Leaders tend to be cautious of those who under-communicate, and the usual consequence is that they are given less areas of responsibility. If giving you an area of responsibility means they'll never hear a report about it again, why would they want that? Be transparent and thorough when communicating with your leader. Show them that when something is assigned to you, they will receive progress reports. That's how you build trust.

In addition, over-communicating with your leader makes it more difficult for people to go over your head. We've all experienced that one team member who knows that if you say "left," they can go to your boss and get them to say "right." By the time you become aware of what that employee's done, it's too late. They got away with undermining your authority. I make it a point to always get to my leader first. If he is up to date with everything I've reported, he won't ever contradict me in front of my team. Because even if he doesn't agree, I'm the first to hear about it and I can adjust accordingly. When it comes to communication with your leader, both timing and content are important.

Learn to like "humble pie"

At the end of the day, no matter how well we learn to manage, we will probably be reprimanded or disciplined. There will be those days when someone goes over your head, or a misunderstanding causes your leader to place unfair blame on you. Then there will be days when you disagree with your leader's method or style, and there's nothing you can do about that. On these days, take a deep breath and a bite of humble pie. Sometimes you will have to be humble, and admit you were wrong. Sometimes you will have to take responsibility for someone else's mistake. Just remember that it's part of the process. Most likely, your leader isn't intentionally burning you, but at a loss of what to do. Whenever possible, use your influence to help them be better next time, but do so with respect and humility. I promise, it does get better as you both continue to grow!

L E S S O N 9

MANAGING RELATIONSHIPS

There's an old concept that you shouldn't get close to the people you lead. The notion that you should have two different circles: a personal one, and a professional one. And that these two should never meet. If this is true, I'm in huge trouble. The forty plus people that make up our office are a very close-knit group. Because our church is over twenty-four years old, many of the people I lead knew me as a brace-faced teenager. They saw me make at least one, if not a hundreds of foolish and immature mistakes, as I grew to become the person I am today. Separating work and personal life didn't ever seem to be an option for me. Since I took a position of leadership, I've encountered more than a handful of uncomfortable situations. Even as I write this, I cringe thinking about every time I've had to deny days off to close friends or confront family members about their performance at work.

Being completely honest, it is the hardest part of my job. As I mentioned before, according to the conventional guidelines for relationships in leadership, it's completely wrong. Generations before us believed that leaders should keep distance from the people they lead and never become emotionally attached. Yet, as I think about my obviously peculiar situation, I realize that the greatest leaders in the world were those that did not abide by that concept. Leaders who changed the world like Mother Theresa, Martin Luther King, and Jesus were also characterized as being people who cared for their teams. They were leaders who believed, like I do, that it shouldn't be lonely at the top.

Good leadership is inherently relational. To get the best out of the people you lead, you need to invest in them, spend time with them, and unless you are a robot you will develop feelings for them. We no longer live in a day, where bosses hand out orders and people mechanically perform them. Our generation needs to believe in the leader, and the vision in order to give their best. Blurring the boundary lines of professionalism and friendship is scary, precisely because we are most vulnerable with people that we are close to.

At the crux of the "lonely at the top" theory, is that a leader needs to be feared so that he or she can keep team members "in check." We think that if people are too familiar and don't fear us, they will no longer respect us. In reality, fear does not equal respect. The fact that your team members are familiar enough with you to critique your leadership doesn't mean that they don't respect you.

One thing I've learned from leading in a tight-knit, family-like environment is to be vulnerable and allow myself to be seen as a human being, even if I am calling the shots. My team knows when I make mistakes, although it may embarrass me. They know I get angry, that I ramble, and don't always exhibit the most becoming of behaviors. But the advantage of having a personal relationship with them is that they believe in me, so they stick with me regardless.

I do my best to be honest and sincere when I've made a mistake and they continue to give me their best even when I have royally messed up. I have their support because I've invested enough in the relationship that they know my heart.

It may seem counterintuitive but having a team of people who obey without ever challenging or asking questions are not the kind of people who propel you to reach your vision. You need people who think differently than you. They will compensate for your weaknesses. And, as long as they do not cross the lines of disrespect, you need people who challenge you because often it can prevent you from making mistakes. As much as people say "it's lonely at the top" those that have made it to the top have had an inner circle of close relationships. Those that have succeeded knew how to harness their strengths and find people who complement their weaknesses. These are the kind of people you should take with you to the top. These are the people who are worth making lasting connections with even though it can get awkward. In all honesty, this is not all as *kumbayah* as it may sound. There have been times when arguments have ensued and I have had to be firm and give clear direction. My team knows I eventually do what I believe is right, even when it's not the best for them personally. It has stretched me and made me feel uncomfortable as it has the team members I've confronted. But where there is a relationship, tensions can be resolved and offenses forgiven.

To understand all of this it is important to recognize that leadership activities are more horizontal than vertical. Having influence is less about position and more about relationship. Vertical leadership is a style of leading where the leader uses people to go up and down his or her personal ladder of success. These leaders use their position of dominance to make people comply, which automatically puts distance between them and their team. Hence, the loneliness they feel at the top. Horizontal leaders lock arms with their teams. They understand that you can accomplish much more by inspiring people to be a part of your vision. A personal relationship is often unavoidable and can be a good thing that draws you even closer to team members. While it can be stressful to balance and incredibly sensitive, knowing that the people in your corner are genuinely a great support and help is priceless. One of my favorite authors, John Maxwell, says that "people don't care how much you know, until they know how much you care."[4] I have found that to be profoundly true. Remember, leadership is about people. It's about getting to know them, motivating them, and sometimes confronting them, but also appreciating your own growth in leadership, and as a human being. With leadership comes the pain, joy, and embarrassment of simply being human. But isn't it better to know that even while you work on your dreams, you don't necessarily need to be alone once you get to them? I definitely think so.

HAVING DIFFICULT CONVERSATIONS

Throughout this book we've discussed many important facets of leadership. We've learned that leadership is relational, and that it involves influencing others to behave in certain ways. It calls us to establish culture and standards of what will be acceptable in our organizations. In order to accomplish these things, we are going to need to learn how to have real, open, and sometimes difficult conversations. Not every rule you set, or standard you enforce, will be met with instant understanding and cooperation by your team members. The truth is not everyone is going to understand the systems or processes you establish. Even those who do understand may not always cooperate the first time around.

There will be many instances where it will be necessary to confront your team members, peers, and even your leaders in order to clarify your expectations or mediate conflict. I want to make clear that confrontation does not always mean an argument and is not aggressive in nature. The word "confrontation" very often carries a negative connotation. There are many leaders who hesitate to confront people and situations out of fear that they will be disliked or considered rude or unkind. On the other hand, some leaders bull-doze over their team members confronting everyone without considering their feelings. Neither of these extremes is conducive to good leadership. If you fear confrontation, and avoid uncomfortable topics or conversations, you'll find it very difficult, if not impossible, to help your team modify the behaviors that may be damaging to your organization. However, if you aren't wise in your confrontation, you risk damaging your influence. Your team may consider you to be cold, manipulative or just plain mean. Over time it will become more difficult to encourage them to cooperate, or even to remain a part of the team.

It's important for young leaders to become skilled in the art of difficult and sensitive conversation. By learning how to have these conversations, we help to establish a culture of honesty and openness amongst our team members. When we are open, honest and thorough, we allow our team members a chance to understand us. They don't have to guess what we may be thinking or what is expected of them. We are also giving ourselves an opportunity to understand them. We give them the chance to tell us what they need to succeed. While you may feel awkward or uncomfortable at first, you will see that after a successful conversation there is usually clarity, relief, and a sense that future conflict will be avoided. I can't tell you how often I've seen tensions arise from simple misunderstandings. When those tensions are swept under the rug, rather than confronted, it often breeds bigger, more intense conflicts in the future, which is distracting for both leaders and followers.

Many of us grew up in households where interpersonal disputes were not discussed, and we may have very little experience in speaking openly and honestly, especially when our emotions are involved. But, with practice we can actually become quite accomplished in relaying uncomfortable information with compassion, kindness, and clarity. Challenging conversations like telling someone they are under-performing or that their behavior is not acceptable become less stressful as you develop this skill. We do not have to allow things to linger in our organizations without confronting and correcting them. As leaders, it is our responsibility to not allow for conflict to have the power to distract or derail our teams or ourselves. The next time a behavior or situation calls for a difficult conversation, here are some guidelines that can help you make sure the conversation is a success:

Calm down

You may have heard this before, but it is important enough to warrant repeating. Don't confront anyone when you are emotionally charged. If you are angry, hurt, or offended, you are not in the best mindset to have a constructive, mature conversation and it can aggravate an already difficult situation. Take some time to cool off, think, and jot down some notes about how you are feeling. Sometimes when we are angry or hurt, we can blur the lines between personal and professional conflicts. For example, after reflecting, you may discover that the reason why you felt hurt by someone's comment was because it reminded you of an incident that occurred in your childhood. As you realize this, you may decide that the "ouch" you felt had nothing to do with the person who made the comment at all, and that a confrontation isn't even necessary. If we don't take the time to process our feelings, we risk exacerbating the conflict. When we fail to reel-in our emotions, we often say things we don't mean, and things slip out that we cannot take back.

Prepare

It may seem strange to prepare for a conversation. We tend to think of conversations, especially with people we know as being more genuine if we just "speak from the heart." However, many of us get slightly nervous when dealing with sensitive topics. So, to avoid leaving out important details, or adding irrelevant ones, I take a notepad with me when I am going to confront a team member or co-worker. On my notepad, I jot down the main items I'd like to cover in the conversation, as well as the preferred outcome of the meeting. Before we meet, I ask myself-- *What do I think the problem is? Is this the correct person to speak to about this issue? What am I asking for? What am I willing to compromise in order to find a solution to the problem?* These questions help give an objective to the conversation. Sometimes, we enter into a conversation without knowing what we are expecting from the other person. If we don't know this, how can we communicate it to the person sitting across from us? Once I have determined the objective of the conversation at hand, I make a simple guideline of the items I would like to be address. I follow these guidelines throughout the conversation.

Be specific

One thing that can make a difficult conversation a bit easier is to give specific examples of what you are speaking about. This makes it easier for the person to understand why you feel the way you do, and harder for them to dismiss your observations. For example, it can seem unfair to the listener to hear that they have been underperforming with no proof, or clarification as to what that entails. It may seem to be more efficient to make sweeping statements than to be focused on the specifics, but this may backfire. Rather than simply delivering the message that they are underperforming, explain how. Perhaps they have missed deadlines for three specific projects. Mention each one and mention dates. Don't be afraid to enumerate them, and be thorough and detailed in your observations. This should be easier if you've prepared beforehand, and if you have taken the time to cool down. It is usually when we are angry that we spew out wide-sweeping accusations and unhelpful words like "never" and "always."

Focus on the root

Although you want to be clear and specific in your conversations, remember to focus on the root of the issue. Sometimes these specifics are just side-effects of a larger problem. For example, perhaps a team member has been making snide remarks about you. In your conversation with him or her, remember not only to address the remarks themselves, but also that they represent a lack of respect for your leadership. It can be tempting to gloss over a conversation and not dig deeper into the basis of the conflict.

However, if the root of the conflict is not addressed, it is probable that the same conflicts will continue to arise in the future.

Be humble

It can be very difficult for the people we are communicating with to understand us if we aren't being transparent. Leaders tend to make the mistake of wanting to initiate confrontation, but then shy away if it seems that their own insecurities are about to surface. Sometimes we do this because we want to maintain an air of superiority or because we are too prideful to admit that we were partially at fault for the conflict. In an attempt to guard ourselves, we sometimes leave out information or veer away from certain topics. Our body language can send the message that we are only willing to blame the other person, but not to listen to them.

Doing this, however, makes solving conflict much more difficult, and sometimes even impossible. When confronting another person, it is only just that we be willing to have an open dialogue, which may include that we be confronted by that individual as well. Now, this doesn't mean that we have to allow anyone to disrespect us. It simply means that in every confrontation we need to also allow the other person to speak, and we need to listen. We have to be open to compromising, and taking responsibility for our contribution to the problem. If the leader does not set the example of humility and transparency, it's very unlikely that the conflict will be resolved or that the situation will have a positive outcome.

Find a solution

Finally, do not allow the conversation to end without a plan for moving forward. Once both parties have had an opportunity to be heard, propose a plan to modify the behavior or change the circumstance. Just as you have been specific about the problem, be specific with the solution as well. For example, rather than saying the team member is going to do better, give him or her specific tasks they must do to improve. Perhaps they can take a training, adjust their schedule, or make some other change that will give them a better chance to succeed. Also, allow them to make suggestions or requests for things they need from you or the organization. Make a specific agreement of what actions will be taken. Once you have agreed on a solution, set a time frame for following up and making sure that both you, and the other person are sticking to your end of the deal.

WORKING WITH YOUR STRENGTHS

I've heard it said that leadership is both an art and a science. Like other sciences, there are facets to it that involve large amounts of logic, strategy, measurement and precision. These are the sides of leadership that require knowing where to place an individual within a team, how to develop an execution plan or budgeting resources. Like the other arts, however, there are components of leadership that require a freedom of mind. Creativity that theoretically can't be learned but that can be developed over time. These are gifts like learning how to inspire, how to motivate, and how to stir people's hearts to believe in your vision and want to come along for the ride. Though great leadership takes both, it's my experience that most leaders tend to be more one than the other: the artist or the scientist.

For me, personally, I've always been drawn to the "people-aspect" of leading, like an artist. It's a talent that takes more intuition than brain power. I like to get to know people and motivate them to improve. This ability to communicate, relate to people and gain their trust comes naturally for me.

The sciences, on the other hand, never came too easily

for me. Although I've acquired some skills over time and through practice, they are still vastly more difficult for me to navigate. At the beginning of my leadership, I thought constantly about my areas of weakness and the things I couldn't do as proficiently as others. I noticed that while I excelled when it came to speaking and teaching, I simply wasn't as good as some of my peers at managing budgets, crunching numbers, or handling details. Although I'm naturally wired to see things on a big scale, I spent a long time trying to become the kind of person who could remember technicalities and specifics. To me, the "scientists" looked smarter, more efficient, and like better leaders than I was.

It wasn't until a few years ago that I started to consider my strengths. I mean, sure I was forgetful, loud, and a little goofy but I was also outspoken, decisive, and loved to speak in front of crowds. It dawned on me that while there were a million things I could not do, there were also many things I could do that others were terrified to do.

Too many young leaders focus on their weaknesses and forget to build on their strengths. We make images in our minds of what a leader should look like. The picture we have may be staunch and strict or carefree and loving, based on what we've seen modeled for us. Then we struggle to fit into the mold we've created in our minds. Somehow we believe that the best way to achieve greatness is to deny our natural bent and transform ourselves into cookie cutter CEO types. But real life is showing us that this is not true. If you look around, there are leaders in every field that look different, act differently, and have totally different leadership styles. If you like behavioral sciences, or studying personality types, you'll see that there have been powerful and successful people of every single type. Some calculated and refined and others wild-eyed and borderline barbaric. They just learned to work with what they had. No one person can be good at everything and trying to be will only distract you from becoming great at the things for which you have natural potential.

In my case, I realized that I can be a great speaker. I'd love it if I were able to exclusively work with words, and my imagination. Those things come easy for me. In fact, when you are doing something you have a natural talent for, it's usually fun and doesn't feel like work. I could choose to invest my time improving my weaknesses, but I'd probably become very frustrated. Yet a person gifted in those areas would do those tasks effortlessly.

So, I will leave you with this very useful piece of advice that was once given to me: "Build on your strengths and staff your weaknesses." Don't spend a significant of time trying to master skills for which you are simply not gifted. Instead, maximize on your strengths. Cultivate the things you are good at, things that you know will give a good return on the time and money you invest.

When it comes to your areas of weakness, of course you should try to improve on them if and when they become a roadblock to your success; but, otherwise, staff them. Find people that you can partner with, that are good at the things you lack. On my staff I have a few math whizzes, detail gurus, and budget ninjas. I rarely worry about these things because while I oversee them, these staff members are more efficient and knowledgeable in those areas. The best part is that they like that stuff!

They are just as thankful that they get to do those things all day, as I am that I don't.

The other day we had an interesting conversation in my office relating to this. Someone asked "whose job, other than your own, would you do well, and whose job would you totally mess up?" We all laughed as we pointed out how much we would hate each other's jobs, simply because it would be so difficult for us to do them. We realized through this exercise that we were all good at what we did because we were placed in the right roles. As I mentioned before, leadership is both an art and a science. While any one of us can be great at certain aspects, no one leader can be great at all things. Building a successful team, organization, or ministry takes nerds and show-offs, "creatives" and business-types, and is an overall a team effort.

As a leader, you will have opportunities to learn and develop skills as you grow in your role. However, I hope that after reading this, you will no longer feel pressured to make yourself something you are not. Whatever personality type you are and whatever talents you possess; you are of great value. There are things you can do that no one else can do! Make time for those areas where your strengths lie by allowing your friends, your team, and your staff to support you.

MAKING AN IMPRESSION

S tudies show that people create their opinion of you within the first few seconds of meeting you. Whether you are meeting a new co-worker, employee or boss, you should keep in mind that the instant you meet, their brain begins to form assumptions, solely based on your appearance. It may seem unfair, but they will be silently assessing who you are based on your presentation, and what they decide in those moments will be hard to undo. Now, I know that we are all more than our appearances. And I by no means want to put anyone down because they don't look or dress a certain way. But the harsh reality is, that we communicate with our appearance and the way we present ourselves. So what are you communicating?

I'm not talking about whether or not you are attractive, because this is of little significance in leadership. But ask yourself if the person in the mirror looks capable, smart, and confident or sloppy and disorganized. Your physical presentation can work in your favor or work against you. This is especially important for those of us in our 20's and early 30's trying to "lead up," that is, leading older, more mature team members. I often hear young leaders complain that the older members in an organization do not take them seriously, but when I see how they present themselves, I have an idea why. People assume that you will lead them in the same way you lead yourself, and your appearance is an indicator of your discipline and attention to detail. If you seem sloppy, lazy or unprepared, you may be communicating to others that you will be careless with their time, disorganized in your planning, and forgetful with your promises. However, if even at a young age you can show your team that you are confident, well-dressed, and put-together they will assume you can get the job done.

Why is this so important? If people are getting the wrong impression of you, you may have to invest valuable time to change that image and regain their respect. It is so much more efficient to have good presentation and give a good impression from the beginning. As a manager, I often have to interview young people for employment opportunities. While I do not consider myself old-fashioned or very conservative, I look at their appearance and body language as an indicator of how they will work. If you find yourself needing a little help in this area, here are some things your appearance may be saying about you.

Showing too much skin

What it says about you: Showing too much skin can mistakenly communicate a lack of decorum. You may appear to be attention- seeking and superficial, wanting people to focus on your "sexiness" rather than on your skills and mental capabilities. This will cause people to question your competency. It may also cause male co-workers to treat you as an object and not respect you for the intelligent person you are.

Alternative: Cover up! Regardless of the weather, it is never appropriate to wear shorts, show cleavage, or too much leg in the office. You want the focus to be on your whole person, your personality and intelligence, not on your body. The rule of thumb for a "business casual" skirt or dress is to be no more than two inches above the knee. Tops should avoid showing any kind of cleavage or midriff.

Being overly trendy

What it says about you: It says to older team members that you may still have a lot of growing up to do and that you might not have developed the maturity to put together an appropriate wardrobe. This can make you seem frivolous and silly, especially if you are a young leader. They may think you're cute, but not take you seriously.

Alternative: I support wearing what is in style, and am not going to suggest twenty-five-year-olds start dressing like they just hopped off the Mayflower! But I would recommend toning down youthful pieces by mixing them in with more classic ones, and saving really trendy styles for after work. The office for example, is not the best place for those awesome combat boots, or blue glitter eye shadow. You want to communicate that you are mature enough not to be shouting for attention with your wardrobe.

The "I woke up like this"

What it says about you: When you wear overly causal clothes or rock the "I just rolled out of bed" look, it can say to others that you are careless, lackadaisical and probably woke up late. It may seem as though you lack purpose, vision, and basic time-management skills. People will think, "this person probably lets things fall through the cracks".

Alternative: Always aim to look polished and well-groomed. The bohemian look is good for the weekend; it may be fit for relaxing but not always for leading. Keep your hair groomed and your fingernails polished and neat. If you can, throw on some makeup simply because it shows you did a little extra to look good. These things communicate excellence, and attention to detail.

Ill-fitting or wrinkled clothes

What it says about you: Clothes that don't fit properly or are wrinkled communicate a lack of self-awareness. If clothing is too tight, it doesn't look sexy. On the contrary, it tells others that you aren't aware of how things fit you, or that you may have gained some weight and didn't notice. In the same way, overly loose clothing can look sloppy.

Alternative: Pay attention to the fit of your clothes. This may require that you have to periodically replace them. Clothes that fit well will not only communicate professionalism, but will make you feel more confident.

Of course, every setting will have different standards of what is acceptable and what is not. For example, many start-ups or small companies tend to have more casual atmospheres. While these comments and suggestions are geared towards a typical office or workplace, I hope you consider applying this lesson wherever you have a leadership role or aim to influence others. Looking clean, well-groomed and appropriately dressed will help you put your best foot forward!

LESSON 13

BECOMING MORE THAN A BOSS

I'm sure all of us can identify with having a bad boss who made us hate coming to work every day. It can be extremely frustrating to work with someone who we can't understand or doesn't make an effort to understand us. Unfortunately, there are too many of these. According to recent studies, three out of four employees in the United States report that their boss is the most stressful part of their job and 65% of employees said they would take a new boss over a pay raise.[5] Yes, they would actually turn down money just to get away from someone who is supposed to be helping them grow. I consider a bad boss, to be a leader that is not doing their job.

Let me clarify the difference between what most people call a boss and a leader. A boss can be anyone in a position of authority. Be it a manager, supervisor, director, duke, or emperor, it really doesn't matter. Anyone can be a boss. But a boss becomes a leader *only* when he or she is able to do just that--lead. To lead means that people are willing to follow your vision, goals, and direction. If you lead well, they won't be pulling their hair out as they do this. The truth is, the world doesn't just need bosses, it needs leaders who can get things done without zapping the energy out of people who are their most valuable resource. As I've reflected on this principle, I've observed how people around me lead their teams. Some are obvious leaders; others are only bosses. There are a few signs that can help you recognize the difference:

The boss speaks, the leader listens

Some bosses are always talking. In fact, bosses often spend *so* much time talking that they have no idea what the people under them need, what they think or what they can offer. Bosses give orders and tell people exactly how things should be done. Leaders give team members an opportunity to participate in the thinking and planning process. They understand that people are more likely to be enthusiastic about ideas they help create and are more likely to support them as a team player. Leaders also listen to their team's concerns. Even if listening makes them uncomfortable. They consider it an opportunity to show they care. Statistics say that 50% of employees who don't feel valued will find a new job within the year.[6] Imagine how few would move out of their positions, if leaders were allowing their employees to be honest when they're offended, and share when something makes them uncomfortable or less productive.

The boss gives instruction, the leader gives vision

Bosses tell you what to do without explanation. As a result, the team remains robotic and unmotivated. Leaders inspire you and tell you why you should follow their direction. The best teams are those where everyone is working towards something they believe in. This is done best when the team has been given a vision to inspire them. That's why a leader must communicate the vision. They share desired outcomes and goals with their team and discuss how these can be accomplished. When a team has bought in to the big picture, they will give 100% to see that picture come to life. Otherwise, all they experience is someone barking orders at them.

The boss is out, the leader is in

A boss is outside of the team. Established rules and standards don't seem to apply to them. But the leader is *part* of the team. Leaders not only talk the talk, they walk the walk. This is also part of communicating the vision. While bosses may be considered to be hypocritical, leaders live what they preach. Every rule and standard they establish is one they are also willing to abide by. Furthermore, a leader is present with their team. Team members know that he or she is available, connected, and willing to help.

The boss judges, the leader measures

Bosses tend to focus on whether or not people are working "hard enough." This is an unreasonable way of evaluating their team members. Leaders measure outcomes and accomplishments. Bosses micro-manage and fuss about whether or not employees have gone to the bathroom too many times. They are looking at individual behaviors and probably missing what is really important. The only real way to determine whether an employee is being productive is to measure the work product objectively: *What were the goals agreed upon for a set period of time? Were they reached? If they were not completed, why?* Some employees can do twice as much with half the effort as their peers. Others can do their best and produce a little less than their co-workers. In the end, the leader's job is to make sure everyone is reaching their own individual potential and learning to improve productivity, not harassing them about how to spend every minute of their day.

The boss is feared, the leader is respected

Because bosses tend to ignore feedback, give orders, and place themselves outside the team, they also tend to be feared. The problem with fear is that it's a terrible motivator. While it may seem to work for a period of time, it eventually turns even the most positive teams into grumblers and complainers. No one wants to work with someone they fear, but everyone wants to get behind a leader they respect. Doing things like listening to your people, giving them opportunities to use their talents, and casting vision for the team gives reason for members to respect you and give their best every day. Granted, being a bad boss is often like having bad breath, everyone knows it but you. I encourage you to examine yourself in your different positions of authority, even if it's a leadership role at home as a parent or a spouse. Are you using that position to cause others to grow? Or are you being considered *just* a boss?

AVOIDING BURN-OUT

S tress is a dangerous enemy in every arena of our lives, and leadership is no exception. Still, it's not uncommon for young leaders to place their own mental health and self-care at the bottom of their priorities. With all the passion, strength and energy of youth, we can sometimes neglect to take care of ourselves. We can disregard the need to rest and become overwhelmed by the responsibilities that come with leadership. However, it's important to remember that leadership should fuel you, not consume you. It's unfortunate that many who think they are being effective, end up burning out. They give up in a short period of time because they failed to take care of themselves. Let's be real, stress-triggered headaches, mood swings, or ulcers are not exactly going to help you reach your goals. And while it may seem that long working hours with little or no breaks result in greater productivity, it can cause stress and anxiety that will weaken your impact in the long run.

So, let go of the old-school idea that you are only productive if you are putting in 60-hour-work-weeks or even pulling all-nighters. The truth is, if you are truly efficient, you will accomplish more in less time through proper planning and organization. There are plenty of ways to manage your time in order to take care of yourself, enjoy your family, and be a balanced, well-rounded person.

I have been a leader for some time now. I manage a staff of over forty people, and a ministry of thousands. While there have been stressful seasons and difficult situations, such as large scale projects and tight deadlines, I've learned to make time for myself, devote time to be with my friends and family and enjoy a life apart from work. It's a must! After all, if I allow myself to be over-worked or over-stressed I will only weaken my impact. If I weaken myself, I also weaken my team and everything I do. Many young leaders forget that taking care of themselves is not a selfish act. It's the key to their longevity and success as a leader.

Stress is something we can stay on top of by monitoring it. Keeping in mind that while our jobs, our teams, and our missions are important to us, a balanced, agenda is necessary. This way, there is more than enough time to do everything we need to without burning ourselves out. Not everyone is stressed by the same things. For some people a missed deadline is little more than a detour in their plans. For others, it can be the source of massive anxiety. It's important to make a self- assessment and identify what triggers your stress so that you can take preventive measures to avoid those things when possible. For example, if you know you don't work well with short deadlines, learn to make timelines that give you ample time to go at your best pace. If you discover that you need more sleep to be on your game every day, schedule your time in a way that gets you in bed when needed.

Moreover, in the same way that your stressors will be unique to you, your de-stressors will probably also be unique to you. Some years ago I discovered that one of the ways I can keep myself from mental exhaustion is to allow myself one hour of "quiet time" when I get home each day. That means one hour of no phone, no chores, and no talking other than perhaps a casual conversation with my husband. This hour helps me disconnect and turn off my racing brain so I can start to relax. I noticed that if I don't have that time to unwind, I don't sleep well. Now, this relaxation process may not work for everyone. That hour of un-winding time, for a morning person who prefers to get to bed earlier might actually be stress-inducing. They may rather get things done so that they can get to bed or de-stress by going for a run. If stopping for a whole hour to do nothing is not for you, then it may actually create more stress than if you had stayed at the office a while longer.

That's why it's important to learn about what can help you, specifically, to de-stress. If you aren't sure, try taking a personality quiz on the internet about how to de-stress. There are so many websites that can help you narrow down what your preferences are based on some of your personality traits. Once you get some ideas, put them to the test, and see what works for you.

Final Thoughts

As this book comes to a close, I want to mention the importance of taking time to appreciate and celebrate how much you've grown. One of the characteristics of leadership is the propensity to hope and dream. Leaders see into the future. Leaders envision. Leaders aspire, and they want move to the next level. It seems that as soon as we get close to achieving one of our goals we come up with another, bigger goal. And usually, we start dreaming about ten new things before we've even accomplished the first. This ambition is what keeps innovators relevant, and what keeps activists passionate. For these leaders, there are always new frontiers to explore. They move on to bigger challenges, sometimes without a moment of rest in between projects or goals.

This inexhaustible passion is what makes a great leader. In fact, I personally believe that dreams should be BIG, big enough to be a challenge to accomplish. When we are passionate about our dreams, we get absorbed in them and it fuels us to move forward. This is a beautiful and fulfilling process, but it can become a negative one if we forget to stop and celebrate progress.

Even if our drivenness leads us to blaze ahead and seek out the next challenge, or possibly to wallow in the disappointment of not having achieved our goal, a lot can be said for stopping to appreciate what we *have* done. Because I am a realist, this isn't always easy for me. Stopping to applaud progress or be grateful isn't necessarily the first thing that comes to mind when I'm on a never-ending quest to accomplish projects and achieve goals. But when I really consider it, this short and seemingly wasteful time to stop and be proud of myself is an essential part of my journey.

We as leaders often sell ourselves short, and have moments of insecurity. We can compare ourselves to others, and wish we were closer to accomplishing our goals. Sadly, leaders do not always have someone to motivate them, encourage them, or give them positive feedback. We are usually the ones who give affirmation, but we don't always get it. If we think about it, though, celebrating our own progress is a way to affirm ourselves and give ourselves a much needed pat on the back. Taking a few minutes each day to think back on where you were, how much you have grown, or even the fact that you made it through some challenging situations, can give you a little push forward. As leaders, it can be easy to get caught up in the things that still have to get done. Frustration and regret are common themes among many of the leaders I talk to. Frustration, however, can lead to a pattern of unhappiness, which is contagious and can hurt our teams. But, perhaps if we learn to affirm ourselves, we will be better at affirming our teams. Learning to be content with our progress brings us peace.

As you make strides to learn each of the lessons I've outlined, make sure you cut yourself a little slack along the way. You aren't perfect and you don't have to be. You're young, you're learning, and you'll get there one day!

Acknowledgements

I want to give a special thanks to the team that worked so hard to put this book together, make deadlines, and not kill me even with all my craziness and perfectionism! Thank you for giving your all to make this project a reality, and for complementing me in all my areas of weakness.

Thank you Sherlyn, for the commitment and oversight you provided for this project as if it were your own. Thank you Mari, my oldest friend, who gave me feedback and helped me compile these lessons. Shout out to my sister, Jessie for catching all my commas and run-ons! I'm grateful to you Janessa, for becoming a graphic designer exactly when I needed one, for giving your all and saving the day!

Best of all, thank you Rico, my amazing husband. You believe I can do anything and everything, and tell me every day. I am so thankful God made us a team!

Works Cited

Covey, Steven. *The Seven Habits of Highly Effective People* . New York: Simon and Schuster, 1989.

Fermin, Jeff. "8 Unsettling Facts about Bosses." 25 January 2015. *Huffington Post* . 30 April 2016. <http://www. huffingtonpost.com/jeff-fermin/8-unsettling-facts-about-_b_6219958.html>.

Groeschel, Craig. "Executive Pastor: Life.Church." *Craig Groeschel Leadership Podcast- Creating a Value Driven Culture* . 3 March 2016. Podcast .

Maxwell, John C. *The 21 Irrefutable Laws of Leadership* . 10th Anniversary Edition . Nashville : Thomas Nelson, 1998 and 2007 .

Endnotes

[1]   (Maxwell)
[2]   (Covey)
[3]   (Groeschel)
[4]   (Maxwell)
[5]   (Fermin)
[6]   (Fermin)

Printed in the United States
By Bookmasters